The Musician's Notebook

Manuscript paper for inspiration & composition

BY MATTHEW TEACHER

RUNNING PRESS
PHILADELPHIA · LONDON

Published by Running Press,
A Member of the Perseus Books Group

Books published by Running Press are available at special discounts for bulk purchases in the
United States by corporations, institutions, and other organizations. For more information, please
contact the Special Markets Department at the Perseus Books Group, 2300 Chestnut Street,
Suite 200, Philadelphia, PA 19103, or call (800) 810-4145, ext. 5000, or e-mail
special.markets@perseusbooks.com.

ISBN 978-0-7624-5647-5
Library of Congress Control Number: 2014937292

9   8   7   6   5   4   3   2   1
Digit on the right indicates the number of this printing

Designed by Corinda Cook
Edited by Zachary Leibman and Caroline Tiger
Typography: Avenir Book and FreeDom

Running Press Book Publishers
2300 Chestnut Street
Philadelphia, PA 19103-4371

Visit us on the web!
www.runningpress.com

HOW TO USE
The Musician's Notebook

song title

(guitar) chord boxes

staff for voice/ melody

lines for lyrics

treble staff

bass staff

guitar tablature

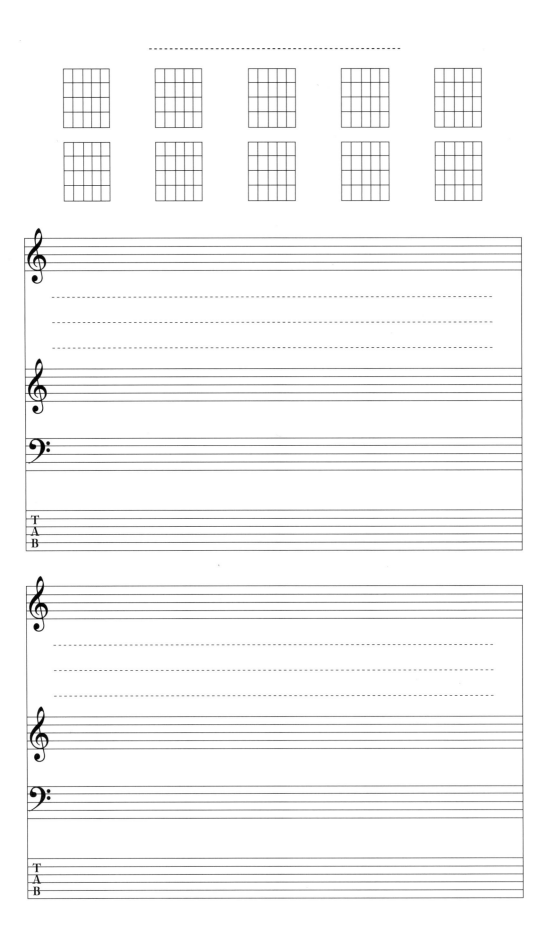

All music is folk music.
I ain't never heard no horse sing a song.

Louis Armstrong (1901–1971)
American jazz musician

Music is your own experience, your thoughts, your wisdom.
If you don't live it, it won't come out of your horn.

Charlie Parker (1920–1955)
American musician

I draw from every situation, everything I come across. That's something I feel really lucky in. I see everything and can apply it to everything else. I make a real easy correlation between things I don't think your average person can make correlations with. I'm always completely thrilled wherever I am.

Michael Stipe (b. 1960)
R.E.M.

The important thing is to feel your music,
really feel it and believe it.

Ray Charles (1930–2004)
American musician

I spend a lot of time with them [songwriters] so they know my
story by the time they write, and it's always the truth.

Rihanna (b. 1988)
Barbadian musician

A composer is a guy who goes around forcing his will on unsuspecting
air molecules, often with the assistance of unsuspecting musicians.

Frank Zappa (1940–1993)
Mothers of Invention

My name is Ella, that's who I am at school, hanging out with friends,
while I'm doing homework. But when I'm up on stage, Lorde is a character.

Ella Yelich-O'Connor (b. 1996)

Lorde

I just wanted a song to sing, and there came a point where I couldn't sing anything . . . nobody else was writing what I wanted to sing. I couldn't find it anywhere. If I could I probably would never have started writing.

Bob Dylan (b. 1941)
American musician

All I try to do is write music that feels meaningful to me, that has commitment and passion behind it. And I guess I feel that if what I'm writing about is real, and if there's emotion, then hey, there'll be somebody who wants to hear it.

Bruce Springsteen (b. 1949)
American musician

I didn't even know what a producer did. I spent two years—day and night—in that studio trying to learn what the hell was going on.

Max Martin (b. 1971)

Swedish music producer and songwriter

I keep a notebook. I also write in my head quite a lot, or sometimes I'll write things out. It's much less a matter of doing the music first. Sometimes when that happens it comes out of a riff. And what's a good riff? Sometimes you'll get locked into one, and in the end you don't come out with a good song, just a riff.

Lou Reed (b. 1942)
American musician

Talk about sitting around for days trying to write songs, in a matter of hours we'd feel we'd been at it too long! John (Lennon) and I were perfect for each other. I could do stuff he might not be in the mood for, egg him in a certain direction he might not want to go in. And he could do the same with me. If I'd go in a certain direction he didn't like, he'd just stop it like that.

Paul McCartney (b. 1942)
English musician

I think in one way I don't even know what kind of livelihood I would have
had without the Internet . . . so much of my channels toward people have been
through free sharing. I think that it's responsible for my ability to tour in
so many countries and different places.

Regina Spektor (b. 1980)
American musician

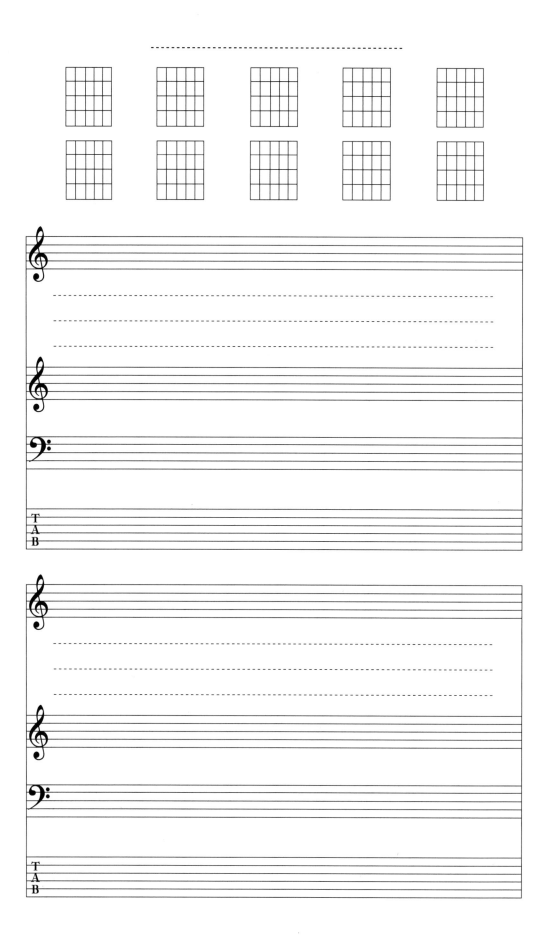

It's just a chord or riff that inspires me and then I go on and see how it goes color-wise. The whole thing just grows like an acorn or something.

Jimmy Page (b. 1944)

Led Zeppelin

I've gone to the guitar because I've had an idea, a line or a riff.
But I don't do that when I start playing . . . I do something completely
different that I had no idea I was going to do. Something inside
that is an uncontrolled wish to express itself, and that's where I begin.

Eric Clapton (b. 1945)
English musician

We're just creating music that we feel has a message that needs
to be told. Whoever likes that, that's all fine by us.

Dan Reynolds (b. 1987)
Imagine Dragons

One day I realized I'd been playing too much in the key of C. So I went to F. When you're a kid, F is the greatest. That's where ["Dream On"] started. It was just this little thing I was playing, and I never dreamed it would end up as a real song or anything.

Steven Tyler (b.1948)

Aerosmith

Those first five or six songs I wrote, I was just taking notes
at a fantastic rock concert that was going on inside in my head.
And once I had written the songs, I had to sing them.

Jim Morrison (1943–1971)
The Doors

*I think first person asserts some gentle authority,
which makes the listener more engaged.*

Neko Case (b. 1970)

American musician

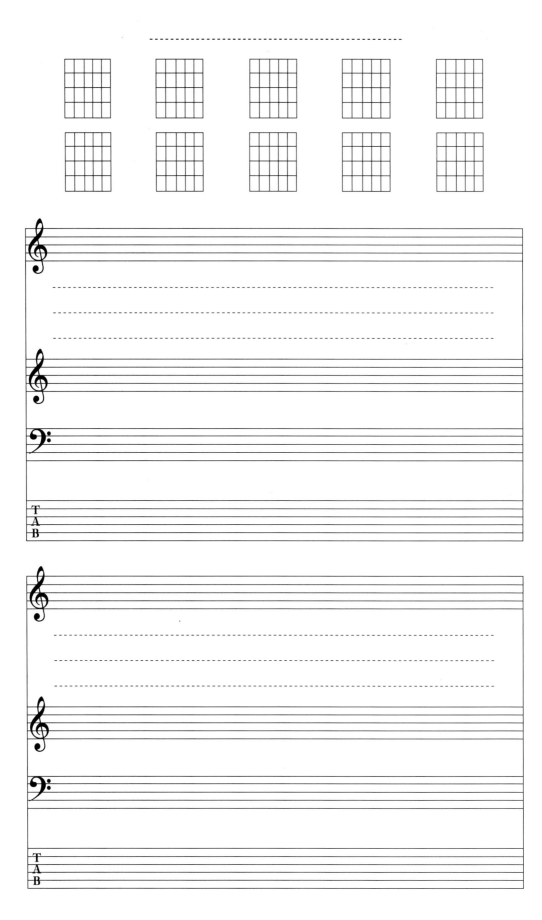

I can't read or write music, so sometimes, in trying to find things, I just stick my hand on the neck . . . I visualize things—sometimes I visualize correctly, sometimes I don't. As a result, some of my favorite things to play started as mistakes.

Stevie Ray Vaughan (1954–1990)

American musician

The way I write my songs is that I have to believe what I'm writing about,
and that's why they always end up being so personal—because the kind of artists I like,
they convince me, they totally win me over straight away in that thing.

Adele (b. 1988)
English musician

You should take that into account when you write a song—
it should be fun to play. When you write a song that's a chore to play,
the performances never sound anything but strained.

Jerry Garcia (1942–1995)
The Grateful Dead

There's only two ways to sum up music: either it's good or bad.
If it's good you don't mess about it; you enjoy it.

Louis Armstrong (1901–1971)

American jazz musician

A great song is more than just words and music.
It's like a thumb pressing against the pulse of living that relates
a simple truth about a very complicated process.

Jimmy Buffett (b. 1946)
American musician

I'm more critical of my songwriting than anybody,
but I've worked really hard in the last five to ten years to improve.

Beck Hansen (b.1970)

Beck

I definitely don't write anything for any audience.
I'm just trying to write lyrics that I think are good.

Fat Mike (b. 1967)
NOFX

To me the success of any truly great rock song is related to the fact that people
who couldn't really communicate in normal ways can quite easily
communicate through the mutual enjoyment of rock music.

Pete Townshend (b. 1945)
The Who

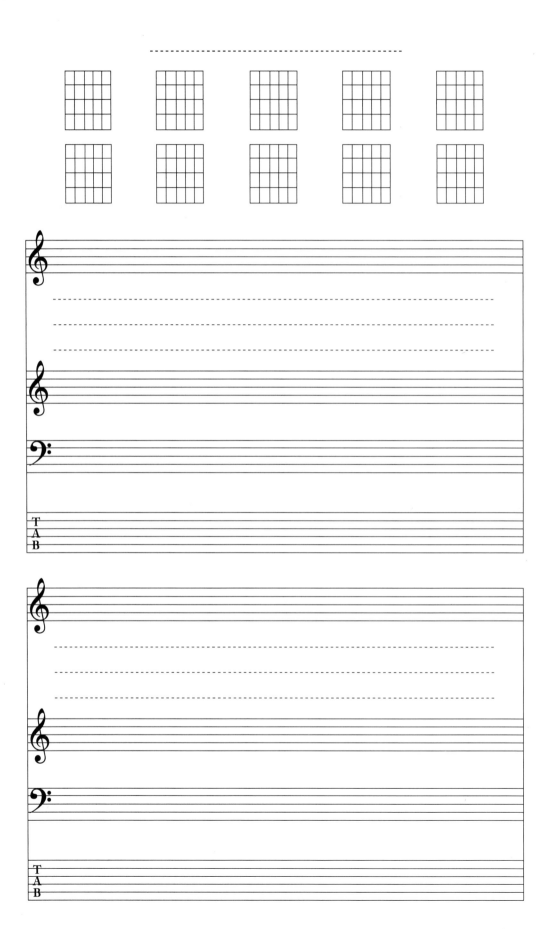

I think a lot of artists spend their whole career writing about the same ideas . . . I think you're drawn to the subject matter you're drawn to. A lot of times, as you change, you approach it from a different perspective and get different insights.

Win Butler (b. 1980)

Arcade Fire

Basically, the whole world is doomed. So the way that I try to make it better . . .
is by playing music that could be spiritually uplifting, that could put people
in a positive state of mind, where they would have the energy to get up
and do something, anything, that's positive.

Flea (b. 1962)
The Red Hot Chili Peppers

I don't want audiences to feel a specific thing—
I just want audiences to feel.

Paul Simon (b. 1941)

American musician

I want to take people to another place in the shows. That's when music really works for me. And that's what I want to do, bring people to a different place. When I'm really connecting, I almost feel a continual state of arousal. There's a heightened awareness.

Sarah McLachlan (b. 1968)
Canadian musician

You have to make something with the belief that on the day it comes out it's somehow going to change everything. It's a very naïve way to think, but you have to be able to believe in it that strongly even though . . .

Thomas Mars (b. 1976)
Phoenix

I think the greatest performances always elude the camera, the tape recorder, the pen. They happen in the middle of the night when the musician plays for one special friend under the moonlight, they happen in the dress rehearsal just before the play opens.

Stephen Nachmanovitch (b. 1950)

American writer and musician

I can't stand to sing the same song the same way two nights
in succession. If you can, then it ain't music, it's close order drill,
or exercise or yodeling or something, not music.

Billie Holiday (1915–1959)
American vocalist

I can't talk about my singing; I'm inside it.
How can you describe something you're inside of?

Janis Joplin (1943-1970)
American vocalist

I feel validated by things that aren't about expectation,
either other people's or my own. True success is . . . the process.

Justin Timberlake (b.1981)

American musician

[Performing is] just a mixture of every emotion that I've ever experienced. It's anger, it's death, and absolute total bliss, as happy as I've ever been when I was a carefree child running around throwing rocks at cops. It's just everything. Every song feels different.

Kurt Cobain (1967–1994)

Nirvana

Ten years ago, when all we had to record on was a four-track, it didn't feel any less full of potential compared to now when we just flip open a computer with twenty-four tracks. Even in a philosophical sense, it's about realizing a context and just getting the most out of a situation.

Scott McMicken (b. 1978)

Dr. Dog

I like to get the heart of every song, find it, record it, mix it, and really struggle to get that magic in.

Adam Granduciel (b. 1979)

The War on Drugs

Music was my refuge. I could crawl into the spaces between
the notes and curl my back to loneliness.

Maya Angelou (b. 1928)
American writer

After silence, that which comes nearest to expressing
the inexpressible is music.

Aldous Huxley (1894–1963)

English writer

If the king loves music, there is little wrong in the land.

Mencius (371–289 B.C.)
Chinese philosopher

Music is religion for me. There'll be music in the hereafter, too.

Jimi Hendrix (1942–1970)

The Jimi Hendrix Experience

I've dedicated my life to music so far. And every time I've let it slip and gotten somewhere else, it's showed. Music lasts . . . a lot longer than relationships do.

Neil Young (b. 1945)
American musician

. . . the blues is for me. It's like a shoe. You take a number seven shoe, you sure can't
wear a size four. You wear the one that fits. The blues fit me.

Muddy Waters (1915–1983)
American blues musician

In my own terms, success is making a living playing music, touring, getting critical acclaim, being recognized, and being able to put out records at a rapid pace.

Kurt Vile (b. 1980)

American musician

In the end I think of music as saving grace for all humanity.

Henry Miller (1891–1980)

American writer